365 Wacky, Wonderful Ways to Get Your Children to Do What You Want

Tools for Everyday Parenting Series

by **Elizabeth Crary** Illustrated by **Dave Garbot**

Parenting Press, Inc.
Seattle, Washington

D1608460

Parenting Press, Inc.
Seattle, Washington

Copyright © 1995 by Elizabeth Crary
Illustrations © 1995 by Parenting Press
First edition

Printed in the United States of America

ISBN 0-943990-79-3 Paperback
ISBN 0-943990-80-7 Library binding

Cover and text design by Cameron Mason
Cover illustration by Karen Ann Pew

Library of Congress Cataloging-in-Publication Data
Crary, Elizabeth, 1942-
    365 wacky, wonderful ways to get your children to do what you want / Elizabeth Crary ; illustrated by Dave Garbot. -- 1st ed.
      p. cm. -- (Tools for everyday parenting)
    Includes bibliographical references.
    ISBN 0-943990-80-7 (lib.bdg.). -- ISBN 0-943990-79-3 (pbk.)
    1. Child rearing--Miscellanea. I. Garbot, Dave. II. Title. III. Title: Three Hundred Sixty-five wacky, wonderful ways
to get your children to do what you want. IV. Series.
HQ769.C923 1994
649'.6--dc20   94-23008
                             CIP

Contents

About This Book

This is an idea book. It has many ideas you can use with children. You need lots of ideas because every child is different. Sometimes the first idea you try may work. Sometimes the second idea you try works. And other times you may need to try many ideas before one works.

Something that works well for another person may not work for you. That's okay. There are enough ideas here for everyone. Different people need different ideas. They have different values for their children. Every child is different in personality and in development. Parents are different, too. Some parents have lots of patience. Some are easily frustrated and don't have lots of time. Your job is to find an idea that will work for both you and your child.

Many people want an idea they can use all the time. There isn't one. That's why this book gives you many ideas. An idea that works today may not work next month. This is because children grow and change. When one approach no longer works, try another idea. Keep trying until you find one that works.

Review of *Magic Tools*

The ideas in this book are made up using the tools and skills presented in *Magic Tools for Raising Kids*. These tools are summarized in five points below.

1. Look for good behavior. Parents usually find the behavior they are looking for whether it is good or bad. If Mom expects kids to fight, she will see more fighting than if she expects to see kids getting along.

Pay attention to desirable behavior. Young children want adult attention. They will repeat behavior that gets attention. Look for behavior that you like and then respond to it.

Praise appropriate behavior. One way to give attention is to praise the child. To be most effective the praise should be immediate, specific, and sincere.

Reward good behavior. Rewards must be given right after a child behaves well. Attention from you is a strong reward. You can also use anything the child wants or needs. Common rewards are stickers, stars, time spent reading a book, or playing a game together.

2. Avoid problems. It is usually easier to prevent a problem than to deal with it. You can avoid problems by making your expectations clear, telling the child what he may do, and changing things.

Make expectations clear. Decide what you want the child to do. Get on his or her eye level. Talk in a pleasant voice. Then ask the child to repeat what you want.

Give two yeses for each no. If your child is hitting the window with a wooden hammer, you could say, "No hitting the window. You may hit the work bench or a pillow instead."

Change things. Move breakable and sharp items out of reach of toddlers. Install coat hooks in a closet so a preschooler can hang up his jacket by himself. Take a two-year-old out for a walk when he is crabby.

3. Set reasonable limits. Appropriate and reasonable limits reflect the child's age and personality, as well as the parents' needs.

Clear rules. State rules calmly and positively. For example, "Touch gently" (no hitting).

Develop consequences. Normal children test rules. Decide in advance what you will do. For example, "Touch gently or play by yourself."

Follow through. Do what you say you will do. If you don't, you will teach your child to ignore you. Without follow-through, all your efforts at setting limits will fail.

4. Acknowledge feelings. Many children have difficulty expressing feelings appropriately. You can help by accepting their feelings and offering different ways to cope.

Active listening reflects both the feeling and the problem for the child. But it does not attempt to solve it. For example, "You are sad that Katie has to go home."

I-messages model a good way to tell someone else your feelings. There are three parts to an I-message. *When*—a non-blameful description of the behavior. *I feel*—how you feel about the behavior. And, *because*—how the behavior affects you. For example, "When milk gets spilled on the rug, I feel frustrated because I have to clean it up."

Ways to cope with feelings. People can use sound, movement, or creativity to calm themselves down. For example, you can talk to someone, or listen to music (sound). Or you can run, dance, or clean (movement) or imagine yourself in a pleasant place, or draw a picture of how you feel (creativity).

5. Reduce power struggles. Some children have a high need for power. There are several ways to deal with this.

Prevention. Notice situations that cause trouble and avoid them. For example, if your daughter demands an ice cream cone every time you pass an ice cream shop, go home another way. Also, physical exercise often reduces stress and power struggles.

Give some power. Let children make some decisions that are not critical. For example, let them choose which clothes to wear.

Use A Better Way. *"My way"* is what I (the parent) want. *"Your way"* is what the child wants. A *Better Way* works for both parent and child. Hunt for solutions that work for both (all) of you. For example, if your child wants to stay up late, and you want him to go to bed now, A Better Way may be to go to bed in 15 minutes.

The purpose of these *Magic Tools* is to give you a variety of ways to solve your problems. No one tool will work well for everyone. These ideas need to be adapted to your situation.

What will work for you?

This book has more than 365 ideas for solving common problems. Some ideas are wacky, some are wonderful. You might have to try two, three, five, or even ten before you find one that works. But that is okay. You will find something that works.

Is this idea reasonable for my child?
Consider both the child's temperament and developmental needs.

Temperament. A child's temperament is his general mood or nature. For example, he may be very active, moody, persistent, loud, or a combination of these and other traits. Even children of the same age differ from one another.

Children are born with these temperament differences. In the hospital nursery you will see some babies cry loudly, while others barely whimper. Some babies kick, squirm, and throw off their covers. Others lie still, hardly moving.

Some temperaments are more difficult to live with than others. If your child is active, loud, persistent, or grumpy, your job will be harder. You may need to get support for yourself.

The ideas that work perfectly for a child with one temperament may fail with another. Think about your child's temperament as you select ways to deal with his or her behavior.

Developmental needs. Children need different things from you as they grow. The two charts following describe children of different ages. Chart 1 looks at the children's needs. Chart 2 shows ages children do common activities. You can use these charts to help decide what is reasonable for your child and how to respond.

Chart 1: Developmental Needs

Age	Child's Job	Parent's Job
Birth to 6 months	**Being.** To learn to live, grow, and trust.	To feed, love, and keep the baby safe. To get the food, rest and support she needs to care for the baby.
6–18 months	**Explore.** To explore his world. To look, touch, feel, move. To drop things, put them in his mouth. To climb in, under, and around things.	To provide a safe home or place for him to explore. To remove dangerous objects and keep special things out of his way.
18–36 months	**Think & feel.** To think and feel. To learn to tell the difference between thinking and feeling. To begin to separate from his or her parents.	To encourage thinking. To tell the difference between feelings and behavior. To accept children's feelings. To recognize "no's" as the beginning of separation rather than disobedience.
3–6 years	**Develop power.** To observe how people (both men and women) get what they want. To decide how to use power.	To model good use of power. To make consequences for misuse of power. To accept children's needs to test rules without feeling personally threatened.
6–12 years	**Develop structure.** To find out how the world works. To find ways of living in it.	To support children as they decide how to get along with their family and friends. To help them make decisions and get *themselves* to follow through.

Chart 2: Developmental Activities

Children learn at different rates. Sometimes children appear to forget one skill while they concentrate on learning a new one. In this chart you will find the average age for doing each task. You will notice how long it takes a typical child to move from needing help with a task to doing it alone.

Ages across the chart: 2 ½ 3 ½ 4 ½ 5 ½ 6 ½ 7 ½ 8 ½ 9 ½ 10

Activity	Help	Remind	Alone
Dresses alone	Help (≈3)	Remind (≈5)	Alone (≈9)
Wipes up a spill	Help (≈3½)	Remind (≈8½)	Alone (≈9)
Brushes teeth	Help (≈3½)	Remind (≈4½)	Alone (≈9)
Puts away toys	Help (≈4)	Remind (≈8½)	>Alone 12+
Washes dishes	Help (≈5)	Remind (≈8½)	>Alone 12+
Feeds pet	Help (≈4½)	Remind (≈8½)	>Alone 11+
Does laundry	Help (≈7½)	>Remind 13	Alone 14+

Ages across the chart: 2 ½ 3 ½ 4 ½ 5 ½ 6 ½ 7 ½ 8 ½ 9 ½ 10

Developmental Issues

Children grow and change. Each new age brings new joys and new problems. Some problems are related to the developmental stage of the child. Three common areas for problems are food and eating, toilet training, and saying "no." While these problems are normal, they still must be dealt with.

Throws food

Reality check:

Know what you want—"I want him to eat his food. I don't want to clean up a mess."

Development—Toddlers often explore food like they do other things. This leads to dropping and throwing food and pouring milk out. Children also may play with food when they are bored.

Temperament—If Ben is persistent and hard to distract, attempts to keep him at the table will be less successful.

Problem:

"Ben, age 14 months, is driving me crazy. He seems more interested in throwing his food than eating it. I want to have a pleasant meal. He just wants to play with his food."

Lots of ideas:

1. Give two yeses. "You may eat the food, or get down and throw a ball."
2. Establish a consequence. "If you throw your food, I will put you down."
3. Change things. Put an old shower curtain, tarp, or large plastic bag on the floor to make cleaning easier.

4. Attention. Include him in your conversation while he is eating well.

5. Notice when he is done eating. Put him down before he throws his food.

6. Keep adult conversations short while he is at the table. Children get bored listening to adults talk on and on.

7. Teach a coping tool. Tell him, "Say 'down' when you are done eating."

8. Reward him for asking "down" by putting him down immediately.

9. Praise him for asking to get down. Say, "Wow. You asked to get down with words!"

10. Clear rule. "Food is for eating. If you throw your food, I will put you down."

11. Follow through. Remind him gently of the rule as you put him down.

12. Acknowledge feelings. "It's frustrating to sit at the table when you are done eating."

13. Prevention. Give him only as much milk or food as you want to clean up.

14. Serve him dinner in the bathtub. Rinse the tub to clean it when he's done.

15. Set a target over a trash basket. Tell him, "Throw the food at the target."

16. Give him lots of opportunity to throw and pour things between meals.

17. Set his highchair in the backyard or on the deck to feed him. When he is done, hose the area clean.

18. Give some power. He may eat better if he controls the utensils. You may ask, "Do you want to feed yourself, or do you want me to feed you?"

19. Let him decide how much to eat. He may already have eaten enough. Chart 3 gives guidelines. If you have questions, check with your child's doctor.

Other books to look at (page 99):

✎ *Airplane, Choo-Choo, and Other Games Parents Play* pamphlet.

✎ *Practical Parenting Tips*, pp. 36–45.

✎ *Your Baby and Child*, pp. 194–206, 291–304.

Chart 3: How Much Food?

Food group	Amount needed each day	Average serving size for children 1 year old	2–5 years old
Protein meat, fish, poultry, dried beans & peas, peanut butter, eggs	3 servings	1 oz. meat or fish 1 Tbs. peanut butter 1 egg ½ cup cooked beans	1–2 oz. meat or fish 2–4 Tbs. peanut butter 1 egg ½–¾ cup cooked beans
Milk & milk products milk, yogurt, cheese	4 servings	½–¾ cup milk ¾ oz. cheese	1 cup milk or yogurt 1 oz. cheese
Grain products whole grains, enriched bread and pasta, rice, corn, cereal	4 servings	½ slice bread ¼ cup cooked cereal ⅓ cup dry cereal ¼ cup rice or pasta	1 slice bread ½ cup cooked cereal ¾ cup dry cereal ½ cup rice or pasta
Fruits & vegetables vitamin C rich dark green & yellow all others	4 servings (total) 1 serving 1 serving 2 servings	¼ cup 100% juice 1 small fruit 2 Tbs. cooked vegetables 2 Tbs. cooked vegetables	¼ cup 100% juice 1 small fruit ¼ cup cooked vegetables ½ cup raw vegetables

(You may make a copy of this chart and put it on your refrigerator.)

Won't use the potty anymore

Problem:
"When Marcy was about 17 months old, she really liked the potty. She used it most of the time. Now, two months later, she wants some frilly pants, but she won't use the potty. I'm afraid she will be like my friend's son. Christopher is three years old and not trained yet.

"It wouldn't be so bad if my mom weren't visiting. She believes Marcy should be toilet trained by now. I don't know whether to back off or to make Marcy use the toilet."

Reality check:
Know what you want—"I want to do what's best for Marcy."

Development—Many toddlers go through a period of "flirting" with the potty. They use it for a bit and then stop. Later, between ages two and three, they become interested again and finish the task.

Average age of toilet training is about 30 months. About 85% of kids are trained before 40 months. Most later trainers are boys.

Temperament—If Marcy is persistent and hard to distract, she may not want to stop playing and use the potty.

Lots of ideas:
20. Relax. She will train herself in her own time.
21. Make training easy. Leave the potty in the bathroom, but don't pressure her to use it.
22. Look on the bright side. It is easier to wash diapers than to clean up accidents on the sofa, rug, or car seat.
23. Make expectations clear. Say, "When you put your pee-pee in the potty, I will get you fancy pants."
24. Tell her if she wants to go potty, you will pull down her diapers for her.
25. Take her with you when you go, and let her sit on her potty at the same time.

Ideas to deal with other people's advice:
26. Refer to an expert. Say, "My doctor told me to wait until she is two years old to start potty training."
27. Refer to research. Say, "Research has found that starting toilet training earlier often makes it take longer."
28. Explain your reasons. For example, say, "I want Marcy trained, not me. When children are trained early it is really the mom who is trained. The mom has to get her child to the bathroom and pull down her pants and wipe her. I want Marcy to be responsible."
29. Acknowledge the person's concerns. Say, "I can see you are really concerned about my decision."
30. Affirm your right to make the decision. Say, "I know you want the best for Marcy, and this is my decision."

When she is interested again:
31. Read her a book about using the potty.
32. Model using the toilet. For example, say, "I need to go pee-pee. I will put it in the potty." When you are on the toilet, say, "Now I am going pee-pee in the potty."
33. Praise her when she uses the potty. Say, "You put your pee-pee in the potty just like a big girl."

34. Give her a choice. Each day you can ask, "Do you want to wear underpants or diapers today?" Respect her decision.
35. Praise. When she uses the potty, say, "You went pee-pee in the potty, just like Mommy."
36. Reward her for sitting on the potty chair. When she volunteers to go, bring out some special "potty toys." She may play with the toys as long as she sits on the potty.

Other books to look at (page 99):
- *1, 2, 3, . . . The Toddler Years*, pp. 75–82.
- *Everyday Parenting, the First Five Years*, pp. 98–101.
- *Toilet Training*
- *Without Spanking or Spoiling*, p. 63.
- *Your Baby and Child*, pp. 315–320, 401–405.

Always says "NO"!

Problem:

"I'm so frustrated. Both the kids I baby-sit say 'no' all the time. Jamie (22 months) says 'no' to everything. No bed. No coat. No trip to the zoo.

"Sometimes she says 'no' and then runs away. Yesterday I asked her if she wanted an ice cream cone. She said, 'No,' then put out her hand for the cone. This morning I decided to go to the park. Jamie said, 'No.' Do I believe her or not?

"I also baby-sit a four-year-old. Eric says 'no' also, but it feels different. He just stands and watches me."

Reality check:

Know what you want—"I want them to do what I ask, at least some of the time."

Development—Jamie acts like a normal two-year-old. She is beginning to separate from you. The "no" means, "I'm a separate person." Try to view her "no's" as a natural part of growing, not disobedience.

However, with three- to six-year-olds the "no" is different. They are learning about power. Eric is probably testing you to see what you will do when he says "no."

Temperament—If Jamie is persistent and loud, her "no's" will be very strong. No matter how loud or persistent, remember with a two-year-old it is normal.

Lots of ideas for two-year-olds:

37. Don't take "no" personally. See the two-year-old "no" as a stage. Remember, she says "no" to *both* good and bad situations.
38. Acknowledge her answer. Say, "Good 'no' saying. And we still have to go."
39. Take care of yourself. If you are rested, it is easier to see the humor in a two-year-old.
40. Give her a choice. "Do you want to walk or shall I carry you?" If she says, "No!" and runs away, pick her up and say, "I see you choose to be carried."
41. Prevent running away. Take her hand before you say it's time to go.
42. Read her body language. Sometimes it helps. If she holds her hand out, it means "yes" even if she says "no."
43. Give a warning before it is time to go. "Soon we'll put our coats on and go to the park."

Ideas to use with 3- to 6-year-olds:

44. Re-think your request. If you really don't care, tell him, "I changed my mind. You may . . ." If you still care, see the next idea.
45. Make the choice clear. "You can walk to the car yourself or I will carry you. Your choice." (Be sure both choices are okay with you.)
46. Follow through. Do what you say. Otherwise kids will learn to ignore you. For example, if you offer him the choice above (#45) and he doesn't start for the car, pick him up and carry him to the car.
47. Make a deal. "Come to the park now, and we can play color bingo when Jamie is napping."
48. Make a game of it. For example, chant "No. No. Ho, ho. When do you want to go?"
49. Do something unexpected. For example, say, "'No' sounds good to me. You can play here, and I'll get a book to read."

50. Find helpful ways for him to feel powerful. For example, "Do you think you're strong enough to carry the diaper bag to the car?"

51. Look for cooperation. When he is pleasant, say, "I noticed how you helped Jamie get in her coat. Thank you."

52. Ignore the "no." Go on as you would if he said nothing. For example, say, "Well, since we are all ready, let's go to the car."

53. Misunderstand the "no." For example, if you asked him to put on shoes and socks to go to the store, when he says, "No!" you could respond, "Okay, you don't have to wear socks if you don't want to."

54. Ask a silly question. For example, "Is Mommy shorter than you?" "Can Daddy ride your trike?" When he says, "No!" you can all laugh together.

55. Reword your request to avoid a yes or no answer. For example, "It's time to . . ." or "Let's . . ." or "Now we're . . ."

Other books to look at (page 99):

✎ *The Emotional Life of the Toddler*, pp. 37–38, 52–54.

✎ *1, 2, 3, . . . The Toddler Years*, pp. 3–8.

✎ *The Toddler Years*, pp. 132–143.

✎ *Your Toddler*, pp. 95–101.

Wiggles during diaper change

Problem:

"Lauren (age 20 months) won't hold still for me to diaper her. Sometimes she kicks me and it hurts when she wiggles around."

Reality check:

Know what you want—"I want Lauren to cooperate while I change her diaper."

Development—It is common for kids to resist diaper changing. Some kids don't want to be interrupted. Other children don't like their space invaded.

Temperament—Active and persistent children often resist changes more than other children.

Lots of ideas:

56. Give her a warning. Say, "In five minutes it will be diaper time."
57. Give her a choice. "Do you want your diaper changed in the bathroom or in the bedroom?"
58. Change her standing up. Some kids like that a lot better than lying down.
59. Change her while she is crawling.
60. Get a safety mirror for her to play with while you change her diaper.
61. Have everything ready before you start so it

takes as little time as possible.

62. When you change her, stand at her head so she can't kick you.

63. Acknowledge her feelings. Say, "I'll bet you feel annoyed at having to stop playing when you are having fun."

64. Clarify expectation. Say, "You need your diaper changed. We can do it quickly if you cooperate. It will take more time if you wiggle. It's your choice."

65. Play "Body Parts" while you change her diaper. Say, "Where is your nose? Where is your hand?"

66. When she is still for a moment, praise her. Say, "Lauren, thank you for helping by holding still."

67. Get some picture books she can look at while you change her. When she gets tired of those books, get new ones. The public library has many kids' books. You can get new books from the library.

68. Give her bells or musical instruments she can only use during diapering.

69. Sing songs as you diaper her.

70. Use disposable diapers.

71. Change diaper before something fun like going to the park or eating lunch. Say, "When your diaper is changed, we will eat lunch."

72. Give her a choice. Say, "It is time to change diapers. Would you like me to change your diaper first or dolly's first?"

73. Make a bargain. Tell her, "When you hold still for a diaper, I will read you a story afterward."

Other books to look at (page 99):
- ✎ *The Emotional Life of the Toddler*, pp. 83–85.
- ✎ *Everyday Parenting, the First Five Years*, p. 75.
- ✎ *Practical Parenting Tips*, p. 48.
- ✎ *Without Spanking or Spoiling*, p. 111.

Safety Conflicts

Parents are responsible for their children's safety—whether they are babies, toddlers, or preschoolers. Sometimes children accept our guidance, often they don't. Many parenting rules are negotiable. Safety rules are not. The following are a variety of ways to handle three common safety conflicts.

Resists the seat belt

Problem:

"Lizzy, my 18-month-old daughter, hates seat belts. She won't accept anything she hates. She screams, squirms, and arches her back every time I try to buckle her in the car seat."

Reality check:

Know what you want—"I want Lizzy to climb into her seat and get buckled into it without a struggle."

Development—Many toddlers and two-year-olds strongly object to being confined in a car seat, high chair, or life jacket. This stage usually passes in two to six months.

Temperament—Children who are physically active or need their own space are likely to object to being confined. Children who are intense and persistent will make their unhappiness known.

Lots of ideas:

74. Look for good behavior. Smile at Lizzy when she climbs into the seat quietly.
75. Praise Lizzy when she cooperates. "Wow! You climbed up and sat down. That's great."
76. Reward Lizzy with something she likes when

she allows you to put her in.

77. Sing a "Seat Belt Song" to the tune of "Mary Had a Little Lamb."
    Now's the time to climb in the car. Climb in the car. Climb in the car. Now's the time to climb in the car so we can drive to the grocery store.
    Now's the time to sit in the seat . . .
    Now's the time to buckle the belt . . .
78. Say, in a pleasant voice, "When you are buckled in, you may have a sticker."
79. Offer two yeses. "You can climb in and look at a special book or you can run for one minute to get your wiggles out and then get in."
80. Change things by making the seat more comfortable. Cover it with a towel or something silky. Borrow a different car seat.
81. State a clear rule. "All seat belts must be buckled before the car moves."
82. Make a consequence. "You may climb into the seat yourself, or I will put you in."
83. Follow through. Put Lizzy in the seat if she doesn't climb in herself.
84. Acknowledge Lizzy's feelings. "You don't like to be strapped in your seat."
85. State your feelings. *"When* I put a screaming child in a car seat, *I feel* tired *because* it takes so much energy."
86. "You can tell me how mad you are in words or shake your hand to get the feelings out."
87. Prevention. Take fewer car trips until this phase passes.
88. Give some power. Let the child choose a "car toy" to take in the car. Toys should be soft or tied to the seat so they can't hit anyone if you stop suddenly.
89. Change things. Have someone else put Lizzy in the car seat for a change.
90. Model desired behavior. Show her how you put your seat belt on.
91. Make a ritual of buckling. Each person calls out when buckled in. For example, "Who is buckled? Count off!
    "One?" "Me," (says Dad as he clicks his seat belt),

"Two?" "Me," (from Lizzy),
"Three?" "Me," (Mom says, as she buckles her seat belt).

92. Distract her by singing songs when she is buckled in.
93. Take a bus or walk to the store.
94. Try A Better Way. A Better Way is an idea that works for both of you. The tool is suitable for children 3 and older. For example, say, "My way is I buckle your seat belt now. Your way is don't buckle it now. What is a better way?" Try to use or adapt the child's idea.

Other books to look at (page 99):
- *1, 2, 3, . . . The Toddler Years*, p. 41.
- *Practical Parenting Tips*, p. 104, 153–159.
- *Win the Whining War and Other Skirmishes*, p. 170.
- *Without Spanking or Spoiling*, p. 107.

Runs away in the parking lot

Problem:

"Robbie (age 2) has been on the move ever since he started to walk. When I take him out of the car he is off and running before I can even pick up my purse. I'm afraid he will get hit."

Reality check:

Know what you want—"I want Robbie to stay near me where he is safe."

Development—It is hard for many young children to stand and wait. Also, they are just learning words like "near," and "beside," so they may not understand them clearly.

Temperament—Some children are very active and will not stay put anywhere for more than a few moments.

Lots of ideas:

95. Make expectations clear. Tell Robbie, "You are so short cars can't see you. When you are out of the car, keep your hand on the car until I hold it."

96. Give two yeses. "You may hold onto my coat or touch the car."

97. Change things. Park on the street and put

Robbie on the sidewalk where he is safer from cars.

98. Attention. Talk to him while you get your stuff out of the car. You can describe what you are doing. (This will also help him learn to talk.)

99. Praise. When Robbie puts his hand on the car, say, "Good for you. You remembered to put your hand on the car."

100. Reward. "You can hold my good luck charm as long as you are touching the car."

101. Clear rule. "Keep one hand on the car."

102. Consequence. "If you let go of the car, I will have to hold your hand."

103. Follow through and do what you say you will right away.

104. Acknowledge feelings. "You're frustrated because I'm not ready to go as fast as you are."

105. Explain your feelings. "I get *scared* when children walk between cars because the driver may not see them and they might get hurt."

106. Offer an idea to deal with disappointment. "You may sing a sad song about how you feel while we walk along."

107. Prevention. Use a backpack to hold your stuff—fill it and put it on before you take him out of the car.

108. Give some power. Tell Robbie, "Hold the stroller still so I can put my purse and packages in it."

109. Give him a car key and let him lock the car door with the key.

110. Let him draw pictures in the dirt on the car.

111. Give him "stickers" to put on the hub caps.

112. Wear a long sash and ask him to hold onto the end.

113. Bring a friend to watch the kids as you get yourself together.

Other books to look at (page 99):

✎ *The Incredible Years*, pp. 183–186, 201–205.

Fascinated with sharp knives

Problem:

"My son Jason, age 4, is fascinated with sharp kitchen knives. While I cook, he watches me. If I turn my back for a moment, he reaches for the knife."

Reality check:

Know what you want—"I want Jason to leave the knives alone."

Development—Four-year-olds are often interested in power. Knives, matches, or guns may seem powerful. Knives may seem interesting because they are forbidden. Or they may be seen as symbols of power. Adults need to help children build a healthy sense of power with themselves, rather than with knives.

Temperament—If Jason is persistent and difficult to distract, redirecting him will be harder.

Lots of ideas:

114. Make expectations clear. "Knives are for grown-ups."
115. Give two yeses. "You can cut bread with a table knife or sit and peel carrots with a vegetable peeler."
116. Change things. Do most of your cooking at night when Jason can't see you.

117. Attention. Talk with Jason about children's safety rules with knives. (For example: "Cut away from you, watch your fingers, stand or sit still (don't walk), stand firmly on both feet so you are stable. Keep knives away from young children.")
118. Clear rule. "If a knife is left out, come tell me."
119. Consequence. "If you touch a knife, you must leave the kitchen."
120. Follow through. If he touches the knife, carry him from the room immediately.
121. Praise. "I'm pleased. You came and told me I left a knife out."
122. Reward. Play a game of his choosing whenever he points out a knife to you without touching it.
123. Acknowledge feelings. "You are disappointed that you are still not old enough to use the knives."
124. Explain your feelings. "*When* a child grabs a knife I get *scared* that he will cut himself badly."
125. Offer an idea to cope with disappointment. Say, "You can imagine how proud you will feel when you can learn to use the knives."
126. Prevention. Eat canned soup for a while, or ask someone to entertain him in another room while you prepare food.
127. Give some power. Let Jason use a table knife to cut cooked fruit.
128. Put up a baby gate keep to him out of the kitchen.
129. Show Jason how to use a vegetable peeler to peel carrots.
130. Tell him what to do. "Keep your hands in your pockets."

Other books to look at (page 99):
✎ *SOS! Help for Parents*, pp. 127–134.

Trouble Between Kids

One challenge of raising children is helping them develop "people skills" with siblings and friends. Most children have more trouble with others when they are tired, hungry, or stressed. Unfortunately, those times are hard for parents, too. The next four problems will give you ideas on how to respond.

Hits the baby

Problem:

"Jessica, age 3½, ignored the baby when he was little. Now that he is moving around, she pokes him or takes away his toys. When I ask her about it, she says, 'It was an accident. I was just playing with him.'"

Reality check:

Know what you want—"I want Jessica to play nicely with the baby. I want the baby to be safe."

Development—Toddlers may hit another child as they explore their world. They want to see what sounds the other children make. They experiment in the same way they shake a rattle to hear the sound it makes.

Preschoolers may hit others to get attention or a sense of power. Adults need to help them find better ways to meet their needs.

Some children have difficulty with a new-born baby. Other children have more trouble adjusting when the baby starts to crawl.

Temperament—If Jessica is persistent and hard to distract, you will need to make clear rules and follow through all the time. Find ways to care for yourself so she does not wear you down.

Lots of ideas:

131. Make expectations clear. Say, "Touch gently. If you want some attention, come ask me directly."

132. Give two yeses. "You can stroke the baby gently or poke a doll."

133. Look for a behavior pattern. When Jessica pokes Charlie, check the time. Write it down. Look for patterns—is Jessica tired, hungry, or bored?

134. Change the schedule. Take her out for a brisk walk late in the afternoon.

135. Give attention. Do something fun with Jessica for 15 minutes while Charlie is asleep.

136. Praise. Notice when she touches Charlie gently. Say, "Nicely done. You touched him very gently."

137. Reward. Give her a star each time she touches him gently. When she has 25 stars, go out for an ice cream cone or go swimming.

138. Clear rule. "Touch gently or play alone."

139. Consequence. "If you poke Charlie, you'll go to your room until you are ready to play gently."

140. Follow through. If she hurts Charlie, take her immediately to another room.

141. Follow through even if she says she's sorry or it was an accident. You can say, "I'm glad it was an accident, and you still are responsible for what your body does."

142. Follow through even if she says, "It's his fault. He grabbed my bear." You can say, "You can find another way to tell him not to touch your bear."

143. Acknowledge feelings. "You feel upset when Charlie crawls in your space."

144. Offer Jessica another way to solve her problem. For example, show her how to distract Charlie with another toy.

145. Prevention. Put children in different rooms.

146. Give some power. Help her find ways to make

Charlie laugh instead of cry.

147. Ask her to make faces at Charlie.
148. Tell her how much Charlie likes her. Point out how he smiles at her.
149. Help her understand what babies can do and can't do. Read *Baby and I Can Play and Fun with Toddlers.* (See below.)
150. Give her words to use to express her feelings. (See below.)

Note: Sometimes children's hitting reflects trouble within the family or at school. If so, those problems need to be dealt with before a long-term solution can be found.

Other books to look at (page 99):

- *All My Feelings at Home: Ellie's Day.*
- *All My Feelings at Preschool: Nathan's Day.*
- *Baby and I Can Play and Fun with Toddlers.*
- *The Emotional Life of the Toddler,* pp. 97–100, 112–119, 165–171.
- *I Can't Wait.*
- *I Want It.*
- *Keys to Disciplining Your Young Child,* pp. 143–147.
- *Kids Can Cooperate: A Practical Guide to Teaching Problem Solving.*
- *1, 2, 3, . . . The Toddler Years,* pp. 15–20, 61–70.

Won't share toys

Problem:

"Todd (age 3 years) wants every toy he sees. He won't share with his brother. Todd doesn't want Brendan to touch his things, even when he's not using them. For example, yesterday he left all his cars out. He was furious when he found Brendan playing with them and started grabbing them away."

Reality check:

Know what you want—"I don't want fighting over toys."

Development—True sharing takes several years to develop. Children go through five stages:

1. Everything is "mine."
2. "Not mine" is different from mine.
3. "Not mine" things have owners.
4. Owners may lend items. (Understands meaning of time, waiting turns, now, and never.)
5. "Ours" is joint ownership.

   Talk to your child about the level he or she is on and the next level up. Trying to skip a level will only take more time in the long run. Freedom from toy battles takes a long time.

Temperament—Some children easily pick up skills for sharing. Other children seem to need a lot of help from adults.

Lots of ideas:

151. Make a rule. "If you leave your toys in the family room, anyone may use them."
152. Offer a choice. "You can play with the cars together or I will put them away."
153. Change things. Buy Brendan a couple of interesting trucks. If Todd wants to use one, he must trade.
154. Attention. Watch the kids while they play pleasantly. Leave the room if they begin to quarrel.
155. Praise. Count the number of times Todd shares. Say, "I noticed you let Brendan play with your truck three times this afternoon."
156. Reward sharing. Give Todd a ticket each time he gives Brendan a truck. When he has 20 tickets, take him out to get a new truck.
157. Make your expectations clear. Say, "You guys settle your trouble quietly . . ."
158. Consequence. ". . . or I will take the cars away."
159. Acknowledge feelings. "You're angry that Brendan was playing with your cars."
160. Show the boys how to play together. For example, Todd could lay magazines or newspapers on the floor to use as roads for the cars. Or, Todd could be the policeman and direct the cars.
161. Give Todd a basket so he can put away the trucks more easily.
162. Offer a coping tool. Show Todd how to find something to trade with Brendan for the cars. Get something Brendan likes (like a music box) and tell Todd to wind it up and offer to trade it for the cars.
163. Prevention. Todd can play *inside* a playpen. That way, if he leaves the toys out, Brendan can't get them.
164. Put any toy they fight over away for a week's rest. When you bring the toys out, remind the children you want them to play pleasantly.
165. Avoid using the word "share." To most children, it means "give it up." Say, "take turns" instead.

166. If things get too frustrating, change the setting. Go for a walk or give the kids a bath.

167. Take care of yourself. Children's quarrels are less bothersome when you have had a good night's sleep.

168. Get exercise. When you are less stressed, you are more able to cope with parenting challenges.

169. Do something you like. When you have some fun, kids' quarreling doesn't bother you as much.

170. Teach your children problem-solving skills by reading *I Want It*. Later talk about what they might do when they want something.

Other books to look at (page 99):

- *I Can't Wait.*
- *I Want It.*
- *1, 2, 3, . . . The Toddler Years*, pp. 57–60.
- *SOS! Help For Parents*
- *The Toddler Years*, pp. 75–79.
- *Your Toddler*, pp. 139–140.
- *Kids Can Cooperate: A Practical Guide to Teaching Problem Solving.*

Teases sibling

Problem:

"I don't know what is wrong with Mikey (age 5). He used to be so nice to his sister Emmy (22 months). Now whenever she bothers him, he calls her names like poopoo-head and dummy. At first she didn't understand. But now she cries when he starts to chant, 'Em-my is a poo-py. Em-my is a poo-py.'"

Reality check:

Know what you want—"I want Mikey to stop name calling, and for Emmy to feel good about herself."

Development—Young children often experiment with name calling. It gives them a sense of power. Some children use name calling as a way to "play" with others. In both cases children need to learn better ways to meet their needs.

Temperament—If Mikey is very persistent, it will take much patience and persistence on your part to help him learn new skills.

Lots of ideas:

171. Interest Emmy in an activity so she doesn't care about what Mikey is saying.

172. Make a game of saying funny names so name calling will lose its power. For example, "Mom

is a poo-pee-pop-pee-pup," or "Dad is a dum-diddle-dee."

173. Check with his preschool teacher to see if something is going on there that needs attention.

174. Give positive affirmations to both children. Say, "You are lovable and capable."

175. Tell Mikey to ask for attention when he wants it.

176. Teach him ways to play with his sister, so he can feel powerful. For example, Mikey can be teacher and Emmy student, or Mikey zoo keeper and Emmy an animal.

177. Play something active that both children enjoy together. For example, "Ring Around the Rosie."

178. Notice what you are modeling. Do you put people down when you are stressed or tired?

179. Make expectations clear. "Treat people kindly."

180. Give two yeses. "If Emmy bothers you, you can find something else to interest her or ask me for help."

181. Find ways for him to feel special. For example, talk about things you did with him as a baby. Or, get a sitter and take him to watch the trucks on a construction sight.

182. Praise playing together pleasantly. "Mikey, you found a pleasant way to tell Emmy she was bothering you."

183. Reward. Look for times he responds kindly and give him a "thumbs up" signal.

184. Clear rule. "Speak pleasantly, or play alone. If you call Emmy names, you'll go to your room until you can act pleasantly."

185. Follow through. Remind him of the rule and take him to his room, if needed.

186. Acknowledge feelings. "You feel annoyed when Emmy keeps bumping into you."

187. Offer a coping tool. Put some special toys in a box. Then say, "You can distract her with a toy from the special box when she bugs you."

188. Notice when the conflicts occur. Do something fun together at those times, like read a book or sing songs.

189. Prevention. Use the energy more constructively. For example, Mom and kids all clean house *together* or run around the block at 5 p.m.
190. Give some power. Let child choose what dessert you will have for supper.

Other books to look at (page 99):
- *Keys to Disciplining Your Young Child,* pp. 54–57.
- *My Name Is Not Dummy.*
- *Raising Your Spirited Child,* pp. 252–253.
- *Win the Whining War and Other Skirmishes,* pp. 77, 179.

Everyday Problems

Most parents try to develop routines to help their day go smoother. As life gets more hectic, children often balk at these plans. When parents look at both their needs and their children's needs, solutions can often be found.

Won't go to bed

Problem:

"Rebecca (age 3½) fights going to bed. She has many tricks to put it off. She won't get in her pajamas. She won't walk into her room. No matter how many stories I read, she still wants 'one more story.' After I leave, she calls that she needs another good-night hug. She pushes me until I finally explode."

Reality check:

Know what you want—"I want to get Rebecca to sleep at a reasonable time without a fight."

Development—Most children give up their nap between age three and four. If Rebecca still takes a nap in the afternoon, she may not be tired enough to sleep when you want her to.

Three-year-olds often begin to try out different ways of getting what they want. You can admire her creativity while you stick to your bedtime ritual.

Temperament—If Rebecca is persistent and loud, it will take persistence and patience on your part to help her go to sleep pleasantly.

Lots of ideas:

191. Explain why she needs sleep. "You need to get sleep so you can have energy to play tomorrow."

192. Offer her a choice. "When you are in bed I will read one book or we can make up one story."
193. Attention. Ignore her delays. Go sit in her room and wait for her to come in. When she does, give her your attention. Describe her actions. "Great, you've come in. As soon as you are in your pajamas, I will read you *two* stories."
194. Encourage her to get in bed promptly. Set a timer for 30 minutes. Tell her, "When you are in bed I will read to you until the bell rings. The quicker you are ready, the more stories I will read. When the timer rings I will finish the story (or chapter) we are on."
195. Praise. When she gets in bed, or her pajamas, promptly say, "I like the way you got into bed so quickly."
196. Clear rule. "In bed and lights out at 7 p.m."
197. Give a warning. "It is ten minutes to bedtime."
198. Do something quiet or dull before bed. This may help her "wind down."

199. Agree on an evening routine with Rebecca. For example, bath, pajamas, in bed, story, good-night hug, and then lights out. Draw a picture of each step in the routine. When she asks for more, tell her, "That was not in our deal," and show her the picture.
200. Develop a consequence. For example, "If you are not in your pajamas at 7 p.m., I will put you to bed in what you are wearing."
201. Follow through. At 7 p.m. ask, "Do you want to walk to bed or to be carried to bed?" If she doesn't go to bed immediately, say, "I see you choose to be carried to bed." Carry her in as gently as she will allow.
202. Acknowledge her feelings. "It's been a fun day and you don't want to go to bed."
203. Offer a coping tool. Give her something of yours to keep her company at night. For example, an old nightgown or sweater.
204. Try prevention. Provide active play during the day. If she's tired out physically, she will fall asleep easier. (Note: Sometimes this backfires.

Some children have more trouble sleeping when they are over-tired.)

205. Give her some power. Let Rebecca decide where she will sleep—on her bed or in a sleeping bag on the floor.

206. Talk about plans for the next day. Explain that the sooner she goes to sleep, the sooner tomorrow will come.

207. Change the rule. "You don't need to sleep, but you must stay in bed. I need to have some quiet time."

208. Do something different. Get a babysitter to put Rebecca to bed.

209. Change the lighting at night. Some children sleep better in the dark. Others prefer a night light.

210. Try a reward. Use a star chart. If she is in bed by 7 p.m. she gets a star. When she has 10 stars she gets a treat, special activity, or special trip.

Other books to look at (page 99):

- *Practical Parenting Tips*, pp. 61–62.
- *The Sleep Book for Tired Parents.*
- *Winning with Kids*, pp.178–183.
- *Without Spanking or Spoiling*, p. 112.

Dawdles while dressing

Problem:

"Brian (age 5) is the slowest dresser on earth. He can't keep his mind on the task unless I am right beside him. If I leave him in his room, he starts to play with his trucks."

Reality check:

Know what you want—"I want Brian to get dressed without my help."

Development—Most children can dress themselves by age five, but more than half still need reminding.

Temperament—It is harder for children who are easily distracted to focus on dressing.

Lots of ideas:

211. Give choices. Ask Brian, "Do you want to choose your clothes today or shall I?" (With a younger child you could hold up two sets of clothes. Then ask, "Do you want to wear your striped shirt or your truck shirt?")

212. Allow enough time. Some children need 20 or 30 minutes to dress themselves.

213. Eliminate distractions. Choose a place that will have few distractions. Tell Brian, "You can

dress in your room or in the kitchen." Set a timer for 10 minutes. If Brian is not dressed when it rings, take the clothes into the kitchen so he will not be distracted.

214. Change things. Buy clothes that are a little big and very easy to put on.

215. Attention. Check on him occasionally. Only comment if he is dressing, or has put something on since you last checked.

216. Praise effort as well as success. For example, "I see you are really struggling to get your pants on. Keep up the good work."

217. Reward success. For example, set a timer for 15 minutes. Tell Brian if he is dressed when the timer rings, you will put a quarter in a jar towards the new truck he wants.

218. Develop a consequence. Tell Brian, "We leave at 8:30 a.m., dressed or not. If you aren't dressed, you can dress at day care."

219. Clear rule. "Dress before you play." If Brian is playing when you check on him, take away the toy.

220. Get dressed together. Shirts, pants, socks, shoes, etc.

221. Make a game. Make a cube (or find a small box). Paste a picture of clothes on each side. Toss the cube. Put on the item that faces up. Keep tossing the cube until he is all dressed.

222. Acknowledge feelings. "You feel frustrated at keeping to someone else's schedule."

223. Prevention. Put all Brian's trucks in a toy box out of the way.

224. Give some power. Let him have one slow-dressing day.

225. Let him pretend to be Superman changing clothes. Make a telephone booth from chairs or a corner where "Superman" can change.

226. Use sweat pants and sweat shirts as pajamas so he doesn't have to change in the morning.

227. Reward cooperation. Set a timer for 30 minutes. Tell him you will read (or play) with him until it buzzes as soon as he is dressed.

228. Reward cooperation. Tell him, "I will set the timer for 30 minutes early. If you are dressed

when the timer rings, we can have a doughnut on the way.

Other books to look at (page 99):

- *The Incredible Years,* pp. 33–51, 187–191.
- *Keys to Disciplining Your Young Child,* pp. 115–118.
- *Without Spanking or Spoiling,* pp. 70, 87–97, 106, 118.
- *Your Toddler,* p. 103.

Won't pick up toys

Problem:

"I don't know what to do about Katie (age 4). She seems to *like* her room a mess. I used to think that she was lazy, but it's more than that. She seems to *prefer* it messy."

Reality check:

Know what you want—"I want my child to know how to clean her room." (Other common reasons are so you can find things, for safety or because you like it neat.)

Development—Your child is typical. The average age children help pick up their toys is 4. They need to be reminded until age 8½. Usually by age 12 they can pick up without being reminded.

Temperament—Some children appear to be naturally neat, others are natural "nesters." With natural nesters you have two problems. One, to get his or her help cleaning up. Two, helping him or her learn to *like* the room clean. The second is the larger task.

Lots of ideas:

229. Make simple rules. For example, "Your room

must be clean before friends come over. It's not safe when it is messy."

230. Offer choices. "Do you want to clean your room alone, or do you want my help?"

231. Work together. For example, "You pick up the cars. I'll pick up the books."

232. Teach cleaning skills. See next four ideas for ways to make cleaning fun.

233. Play the alphabet game. Pick up things starting with A (airplane). Next, B (ball). Then C (car, stuffed cat).

234. Play treasure hunt. Hide stickers (or pennies) under things. Katie will find them as she puts things away.

235. Play "Divide and Conquer." Ask the child to choose one part of the room for you to work on together. For example, the part near the bed. When that is done, the child chooses another part to clean.

236. Play "Genie." Become her assistant. Ask her, "What can I do to help you clean your room?" (You may need to explain you are a baby Genie and only work with someone, never alone.)

237. Change things—trade cleaning. You clean her room. She cleans yours.

238. Give two yeses. For example, "You can clean for five minutes and rest for five minutes until your room is clean. Or, you can clean all at once and get it done faster."

239. Establish standards. Explain what should be done when the room is clean. Draw pictures or make a list. Then have her check your room. (Make sure you make some mistakes that she can find.) When she gets used to checking your room, it will be easier for her to check herself.

240. Praise. When the room is clean, say, "Wow, this looks great. You can walk across the room with your eyes closed."

241. Reward. Give her a star each night her room is clean when she goes to bed. When she gets 10 stars she can invite a friend to stay overnight.

242. Clear rule. "Your room must be clean before you have a friend over."

243. Consequence. "If your room is messy, your friend must go home or wait outside until it is clean."

244. Follow through. Take the friend home if necessary.

245. Acknowledge feelings. Say, "Sometimes the mess feels too big to clean up."

246. Change your attitude. Decide that a clean room doesn't matter as long as the door is closed. (Note: Tell her that you have changed your mind. Otherwise it will appear as though she is getting away without cleaning.)

247. Reduce the mess. Let Katie fill a basket with toys to give to a battered women's shelter or someone who has few toys.

248. Get yourself help. Hire someone to clean her room once a week.

Other books to look at (page 99):

✎ *The Incredible Years*, pp. 33–63, 116–118.

✎ *Keys to Disciplining Your Young Child*, pp. 62–66.

✎ *Without Spanking or Spoiling*, pp. 110, 118.

Whines all the time

Problem:
"Elizabeth (age 4) whines continuously. She starts when she gets up and doesn't stop until she is sound asleep. The whining is worst when she wants something."

Reality check:
Know what you want—"I want Elizabeth to talk pleasantly."

Development—Whining is very common for young children. One- and two-year-olds may whine as they learn to speak. Three-, four-, and five-year-olds often whine when they want something, want attention, or when frustrated.

Whining is so common that one survey found that over half the parents of three-, four-, and five-year-olds reported that whining was a problem for them.

Temperament—Most children who whine are persistent. The persistence is desirable; however, it needs to be redirected.

Lots of ideas:
249. Notice when your child asks for something

pleasantly. If possible, give it to her. If not, say, "You used your pleasant voice. I can't give you . . . but I can . . ." (Offer something you think she might like instead.)

250. Make expectations clear. Say, "Talk pleasantly. I do not like to hear whining."

251. Use humor. For example, make a silly poem:
     Silly you. Silly you.
     The sour whine bug's bitten you.
     Take a drink to clear your throat.
     That's the magic antidote.
     Smile and hand her a drink of water. Then ask her to try again.

252. Ask Elizabeth to repeat the request with a smile. (It is hard to smile and whine at the same time.)

253. Notice if she whines more when she is hungry or tired. Then, try to reduce those times.

254. Be silly. Give her a raisin and say, "Here is a pleasant pill. Eat this and use your pleasant voice."

255. Praise her effort. Say, "Thank you for using your pleasant voice," or "Wow, you remembered your pleasant voice."

256. Help child identify a pleasant voice. Sometimes kids whine so much they don't know what talking pleasantly sounds like.

257. Make a clear rule and consequence. "Ask pleasantly, or the answer is 'No.'"

258. Another clear consequence. "Talk pleasantly, or talk alone. If you whine, I will walk away."

259. Follow through! You must do as you say. If you give in, you teach your child to ignore you. For example, if your child whines, you could say, "That is whining. I am happy to listen to you when you speak in a pleasant voice. I will be in the living room waiting to hear your pleasant voice." Then walk away.

260. Acknowledge feelings. You might say, "You're disappointed that you have to wait for dinner."

261. If Elizabeth has trouble speaking pleasantly, ask her to pitch her voice lower. It is hard to whine in a deep voice.

262. See that she gets enough food, rest, and exercise. When she feels better, she will get less frustrated.
263. When she is pleasant, give her lots of attention. Say, "You are fun to be with."
264. Give some power. Tell her she can have two whines a day that you will listen to. Make one special "whine" card or ticket. Give her the card each morning when she wakes up. Then when she whines, ask if this is her special whine time for the day. If it is, ask for the whine ticket. If not, she needs to rephrase her statement.
265. Give her a star for every 15 minutes she speaks pleasantly. When she gets five stars, read her a story (or do something else she enjoys).
266. Ignore whining. Leave the room if necessary. Try to be casual. Speak to someone else or act distracted.
267. Give two yesses. Say, "I do not want to hear whining. You may whine in the bathroom or speak pleasantly to me."
268. Teach her to calm herself when she starts to get frustrated. She could take three deep breaths or move away from the activity for a few minutes.
269. Take care of yourself. Get enough sleep and exercise so her whining does not bother you as much.

Other books to look at (page 99):
- ✎ *Keys to Disciplining Your Young Child*, pp. 132–135.
- ✎ *Win the Whining War and Other Skirmishes*, pp. 17, 54, 56, 191.
- ✎ *Without Spanking or Spoiling*, pp. 78, 105.

Interrupts me on the phone

Problem:

"Jason (age 1½) wants me the instant the phone has rung. As soon as the phone rings he is there. If I make a call, as soon as he notices it, he says, 'Up, Mommy. Up, Mommy'."

Reality check:

Know what you want—"I want him to play by himself for a few minutes when I am on the phone."

Development—Most toddlers need "emotional refueling." They come and go frequently. When you want to be left alone, they want to stick closer. They need to be sure you are open to them.

Temperament—Some children are easily distracted and others are very persistent. If your child is distractable, use it. If your child is persistent, think about your response ahead of time so you can choose something you can follow through with.

Lots of ideas:

270. Give him a toy phone so he can talk on his phone while you talk.

271. Make a special activity he can do **only** while you are on the phone. For example, play dough and cookie cutters. When the phone rings, get the special toys out for him to play with while you are on the phone.
272. Bounce him on your leg while you talk.
273. Tell the caller you'll call back in five minutes. Give him attention and then call back.
274. Set a timer for three minutes. Tell him you will get off the phone and play with him when the timer rings. To develop trust, stop your call immediately when the timer rings.
275. Plan the calls you make for when he is asleep (nap or night).
276. When he wants up, give him a choice. For example, "Do you want to sit on my lap quietly or play with the play dough?"
277. Let him say hello to the person on the phone.
278. If you are playing together when the phone rings, consider letting it ring. If you decide to answer it, tell him you will be back when you are done. Then set a timer or something so you remember. If you do not return, you teach him he doesn't have to keep his word.
279. Tell him, if he misses you while you are on the phone, he can cuddle with his blanket.
280. Get an answering machine and let it record the message.
281. Give him a back rub while you talk on the phone.
282. Roll a ball back and forth between you as you talk on the phone.
283. Acknowledge his feelings. For example, "It is frustrating to wait while I'm on the phone."
284. Cover your head with a blanket to muffle the noise he makes.
285. If the call is an emergency, put your child in a playpen or crib.

Other books to look at (page 99):
- ✐ *The Emotional Life of the Toddler*, pp. 172–177.
- ✐ *The Incredible Years*, pp. 64–72.
- ✐ *Keys to Disciplining Your Young Child*, pp. 93–97.
- ✐ *Without Spanking or Spoiling*, p. 119.

Public Parenting

One of the hardest times for parents is parenting in public. Many parents who find it easy at home, find it hard to set limits in public and face a tantrum. Even wise, caring parents get embarrassed when everyone is watching. Ideas for four common problems follow.

Won't leave the park

Problem:

"Eric (28 months) *loves* the park. No matter how long we are there, he has a fit when we leave. I have to pick him up screaming and squirming. It is so frustrating I almost hate to go."

Reality check:

Know what you want—"I want Eric to leave the park without a struggle."

Development—The typical two-year-old is rigid and inflexible. He wants what he wants, when he wants it. He has not yet learned to adapt. You can listen to his outbursts knowing that the phase will most likely pass as he grows older.

Temperament—Active children are likely to want to stay at the park. If Eric is also determined and very loud, it may be hard to get him to leave. If you are both calm and firm, his behavior will improve with time.

Lots of ideas:

286. Give an advance warning. "In five minutes we will go." Or, "Two more slides and we leave."

287. Give him some power. Let him set a timer for the time to leave.

288. Do not extend the departure deadline. Leaving gets easier if you are firm.
289. Offer a choice. "Do you want to walk home or be carried?"
290. Follow through with the choice. If he runs away, pick him up and say, "I see you decided to be carried home."
291. Plan something fun for when you get home.
292. Leave a snack in the car to eat on the way home.
293. Plan to get back in time to see *Mr. Rogers* or *Sesame Street* on TV.
294. Praise his cooperation. Say, "Thank you for leaving pleasantly today."
295. Acknowledge feelings. "You like to play at the park. You are mad or disappointed that you have to go home now."
296. Prevention. Take fewer trips to the park.
297. Clarify his choice. "Do you want to leave pleasantly or do you want me to carry you?"

Other books to look at (page 99):

- *The Incredible Years*, pp. 183-186, 201–205.
- *1, 2, 3 . . . The Toddler Years*, pp. 15–43, 71–74.
- *Raising Your Spirited Child*, pp. 185–197.
- *SOS! Help for Parents*, pp. 191–194.

Won't sit still in church

Problem:

"I don't know what's wrong with Amanda (age 3). She can't sit still for five minutes. She slides off the pew and disappears under it before I can stop her. I'm afraid she is bothering the people behind us. It's so embarrassing."

Reality check:

Know what you want—"I want Amanda to sit through the church service."

Development—Many three-year-olds have trouble sitting still more than five or ten minutes. Many school-aged children have trouble sitting still for a whole hour.

Temperament—Children who like to move a lot and are naturally noisy will have a hard time sitting quietly.

Lots of ideas:

298. Plan ahead. Bring some quiet activities for Amanda to do. For example, crayons and paper, dolls, or play dough. Bring some books for her to look at.
299. Sit in the back row so she can move around without disturbing people.
300. Bring beads or pasta to thread on a string.

301. Take her outside to run if she gets restless.

302. Change things. Switch to a different church that offers a children's church program.

303. Let her wiggle during hymns.

304. Give attention. Catch her eye occasionally while she is quiet and smile.

305. Praise. Draw her a smiling face. Or tell her, "Good job sitting" when the congregation stands up to sing.

306. Reward. Give her a piece of sugarless gum if she makes it to the offering without going under the pew.

307. Clear rule. "Sit quietly in church."

308. Consequence. "If you go under the pew, you go to the nursery."

309. Follow through. If she climbs under the pew, pick her up and carry her out, even if she cries.

310. Acknowledge feelings. "It is frustrating to sit quietly for so long."

311. Explain your feelings. *When* someone makes loud noises during church, I feel *frustrated* because it is hard to hear the sermon.

312. Offer a coping tool. Say, "When you feel fidgety, shake your hand to get the wiggles out."

313. Prevention. Ask someone to baby-sit for Amanda while you go to church.

314. Give some power. Amanda can choose whether she wants to go to the nursery or sit quietly with you.

Other books to look at (page 99):
- *1, 2, 3, . . . The Toddler Years*, pp. 101–103.
- *SOS! Help for Parents*, pp. 23–30.
- *Without Spanking or Spoiling*, p. 114.

Grocery store tantrums

Problem:

"I hate grocery shopping. If it's not one problem, it's another. If I put Jenny in the grocery cart, she cries to get down. If I put her down, she runs away. During the few times she stays near the cart, she always wants to buy everything she sees."

Reality check:

Know what you want—"I would like to get the shopping done with no major tantrum."

Development—Almost all parents face this problem with preschoolers. Struggles may be short-lived or continue for months.

Temperament—Grocery store struggles are more embarrassing with intense, persistent children. Children who are persistent and like to move a lot will have difficulty sitting in the grocery cart or walking beside it.

Lots of ideas:

315. Plan the shopping trip when you and the child are rested and well fed.

316. Give attention. Talk to your child as you shop. Explain how you decide what to buy, how you select fresh fruits and vegetables, etc.

317. Help her make choices. Tell Jenny, "You may

have one thing from the grocery store." When she wants something else too, get out the first item and ask her which one she wants to keep. Repeat as many times as needed.

318. Offer a coping tool. Bring a book for the child to look at in the cart. When she is older, ask *her* what she would like to bring.

319. Praise. Notice when she is pleasant. Say, "Jenny, you are talking quietly. It's fun to go shopping with you."

320. Get a treat. Let Jenny choose a piece of fruit. Have it weighed or pay for it. Then she may eat it as you shop. (Also, some stores have free cookies for kids.)

321. Clear rule. "Walk by the cart or sit in the seat."

322. Follow through. When she runs away, pick her up and put her in the cart. Do so even if she screams.

323. Ignore the stares. People who also have challenging children will understand and not criticize you. People who have easy children probably won't understand.

324. Acknowledge her feelings. "It is frustrating to sit in the cart when you want to run."

325. Prevention. Leave the kids with their dad or a neighbor while you shop.

326. Give some power. Let her help by pushing the cart or dropping things you give her into the basket.

327. If things get too noisy, quit. Leave the cart and take the screaming child to the car. Wait for Jenny to calm herself, or go home and come back another time.

328. Talk to her about what you will do when you are done shopping.

329. Decide it's okay. Tell yourself if Jenny is this persistent about getting the cereal she wants, she will get through school if she wants.

Other books to look at (page 99):

- ✎ *The Emotional Life of the Toddler*, pp. 38–54, 85.
- ✎ *Keys to Disciplining Your Young Child*, pp. 98–101.
- ✎ *Raising Your Spirited Child*, pp. 170–182.

Is shy in public

Problem:
"William (age 2½) is so shy I'm embarrassed wherever we go—preschool, church, stores. When my mom comes he won't even kiss her hello. He hangs his head and won't look at her. He should try to be friendly. I don't want him to grow up being shy with everyone."

Reality check:

Know what you want—"I want William to be comfortable around people."

Development—Two-and-a-half-year-olds are not easy in any social group. They tend to be rigid and demanding, each in their own way. As children grow older, they will learn skills that will help them be comfortable with new people and new settings.

Temperament—Some children are "slow to warm." Slow-to-warm kids are uncomfortable with people they do not see everyday. They are uncomfortable in new situations.

Slow-to-warm kids do well when you give them enough time to adapt. Some children adapt in several weeks. Other children take months or even a year before they are comfortable with people and places.

Lots of ideas:

330. Give your child time to be with new people before you expect him to talk with them. This may take up to an hour.

331. Keep a picture of your mother where he can see it. Talk to him about her between visits so he remembers her. Let him talk to her on the phone.

332. Plan to arrive early at preschool, church, or the park so he has a chance to accustom himself to the place before there are many people around.

333. Affirm your child's feelings. Say, "It feels scary meeting new people."

334. Affirm your child's style. Say, "You can take the time you need to feel comfortable."

335. Let him take a "lovey" or something to help him feel more comfortable.

336. Offer two yesses. "When you feel shy, you can take three deep breaths or hold my hand."

337. Decrease the problem. Make sure he is rested, well fed, and has a "lovey" with him when he goes to new places.

338. Explain to people, "It takes William a little time to feel comfortable."

339. Set expectation of success. Say, "William, when you feel more comfortable, you will explore all those new things."

340. Make a "Pleasant Place." Think of a place he likes to be. For example, a comfortable, old reading chair. When you are there, remark on how comfortable it is. Later add, "When you feel scared or shy you can imagine yourself here in the Pleasant Place." Practice going to the Pleasant Place.

341. Tell your mother he needs time to feel comfortable before kissing her. Say, "William needs time to remember you before he talks to you. He will come over when he is ready."

342. Tell yourself, "I am a good parent even when my child is shy. His being here is enough for today."

343. Remind yourself that he will grow fastest if he has a chance to adapt.

344. Slowly introduce him to new situations. Moving too fast will make him insecure. Moving too slow will let him remain "stuck." Get to know his pace, so you can find the right balance.

345. Praise his effort. Say, "I saw you talk to the boy. That was brave."

346. Invite preschool friends over one at a time so he can make friends with them at his own pace.

347. Tell him, "You make friends at your own pace. When you are ready, let me know."

348. Foreshadow new experiences or changes in schedule. Talk over with him what he will do and who he might meet.

349. Have your mother play some of his favorite games with you. When he gets comfortable watching, he may choose to ask her to play again with him.

Other books to look at (page 99):

✎ *The Emotional Life of the Toddler*, pp. 59–79, 100–122.

✎ *Raising Your Spirited Child*, pp. 51–71

Just for Parents

Parenting young children can be rewarding as well as exhausting. You must take care of yourself so that you can take of your kids. If you feel overwhelmed, angry, discouraged, or depressed, you need to change something.

What can I do when I get angry or frustrated?

Problem:

"Sometimes I get so tired or upset that I want to yell or strike out. My dad did that all the time. I don't want to explode, but I don't know what to do instead."

Reality check:

Know what you want—"I want to stay calm."

Development—Young children take much energy. You can avoid much frustration by taking care of yourself. Take care of yourself by getting enough food, sleep, exercise, and support.

Temperament—Some children's temperaments are hard to live with. If your child is active, persistent, and has a negative mood, find ways to get a break.

Ideas for taking care of you:

350. Take a nap when your child does. If he doesn't nap, then have a "quiet time" each day when you lie down together. You can talk, read books, or listen to music.

351. Get exercise each day. Put your child in the stroller and go for a brisk walk, or put on music and dance to it.

352. Eat nutritious food, especially fruit, vegetables, and grains. Avoid snack food like pop, chips, and sweets. Avoid alcohol, beer, and drugs.

353. On weekends, you and your spouse take turns sleeping late.

354. Swap sitting with a friend so you can have one afternoon a week free.

355. Have Grandma take the kids once a week so you can sleep.

356. Get a sitter to come in one or two hours after school so you can sleep or relax.

357. Do something you like each day. For example, read a book, take a walk and smell the flowers, or call a friend.

358. Take an exercise class at a neighborhood center.

359. Do aerobics with a television show.

360. Talk with a supportive friend.

361. Take a bubble bath.

Ideas for getting calm:

362. When you feel yourself getting angry, try a calming tool: take five deep breaths, count to 10 or 25, say the alphabet backwards.

363. Ask a friend how he or she calms down.

364. Separate your feelings from your child. Remind yourself that you are a good person, even if your child is being difficult.

365. Do five jumping jacks. (Jump "open" with your feet apart and your arms wide. Then jump "closed" with your feet together and arms straight overhead.)

366. Turn around and look out the window (or at a pleasant picture).

367. Tell yourself, "I can deal with this. This too will pass. This is just a phase."

368. Tell your child, "I need a time-out. I will talk to you when I have calmed down." Make sure the child is in a safe place, then step away to calm yourself.

369. Imagine you are in a calm, restful place. Let the calm drift through you.

370. Figure out what makes you angry and then develop a plan to change the situation.

371. Call your local crisis line and ask for help.
372. Plan to avoid problems. When you remember to use your ideas, reward yourself.
373. Find a friend or a group of mothers to talk over your feelings and problems with.
374. Remind yourself of the good times and savor them. If you have trouble thinking of good times, ask a friend to help you. Look forward to more good times.

Other books to look at (page 99):
- ✎ *Taking Care of Me*
- ✎ *Woman's Comfort Book*

Other Books to Look At

Airplane, Choo-Choo, and Other Games Parents Play, Washington State Dairy Council, 4201 198th St. S.W., Suite 102, Lynnwood, WA 98036. Free brochure.

All My Feelings at Home: Ellie's Day and All My Feelings at Preschool: Nathan's Day, S. Conlin and S. L. Friedman. Seattle: Parenting Press, 1991 and 1989.

Baby and I Can Play & Fun with Toddlers, K. Hendrickson. Seattle: Parenting Press, 1990.

Emotional Life of the Toddler, The, A. Lieberman. New York: The Free Press, 1993.

Everyday Parenting: The First Five Years, R. Goldstein. New York: Penguin Books, 1990.

I Can't Wait, E. Crary. Seattle: Parenting Press, 1982.

I Want It, E. Crary. Seattle: Parenting Press, 1982.

Incredible Years, The, C. Webster-Stratton, Ph.D. Toronto: Umbrella Press, 1992.

Keys to Disciplining Your Young Child, E. Siegel, M.A. and L. Siegel, M.D. New York: Barron's, 1993.

Kids Can Cooperate: A Practical Guide to Problem Solving, E. Crary. Seattle: Parenting Press, 1984.

My Name Is Not Dummy, E. Crary. Seattle: Parenting Press, 1983.

1, 2, 3, . . . The Toddler Years, I. Van der Zande. Santa Cruz: Santa Cruz Toddler Care Center, 1990.

Practical Parenting Tips, V. Lansky. New York: Meadowbrook Press, 1992.

Raising Your Spirited Child, M. Kurcinka. New York: Harper Perennial, 1991.

Sleep Book for Tired Parents, R. Huntley. Seattle: Parenting Press: 1991.

SOS! Help for Parents, L. Clark, Ph.D. Bowling Green: Parents Press, 1985.

Taking Care of Me (So I Can Take Care of Others), B. Carlson, M. Healy, G. Wellman. Seattle: Parenting Press, 1995.

Toilet Training, V. Lansky. New York: Bantam Books, 1984.

Toddler Years, The, A. Popper. New York: Ballantine Books, 1986.

Win the Whining War and Other Skirmishes, C. Whitman, M.S.W. Los Angeles: Perspective Publishing, 1991.

Winning with Kids, T. A. Warshaw, Ph.D. & V. Secunda. New York: Bantam Books, 1988.

Without Spanking or Spoiling, Second Edition, E. Crary, Seattle: Parenting Press, 1993.

Woman's Comfort Book: A Self-Nurturing Guide for Restoring Balance in Your Life, J. Louden. San Francisco: HarperCollins, 1992.

Your Baby and Child, P. Leach. New York: Alfred A. Knopf, 1992.

Your Toddler, R. Rubin, Ph.D, J. Fisher, M.A., S. Doering, Ph.D. New York: Collier Books, 1980.

Index

Order these books for quick ideas

Tools for Everyday Parenting Series

Illustrated. Paperback, $9.95 each; library binding, $18.95 each

These books are geared for new or frustrated parents. Fun to look at and fun to read, they present information in both words and cartoons. They are perfect for parents who may be busy with school, jobs, or other responsibilities and who have little time to read.

Magic Tools for Raising Kids, by Elizabeth Crary • Parenting young children is easier and more effective with a toolbox of useful, child-tested, positive tools. Learn what to do, how to do it, and what to say to make raising lovable, self-confident kids easier.
128 pages, ISBN 0-943990-77-7 paperback, 0-943990-78-5 library

365 Wacky, Wonderful Ways to Get Your Children to Do What You Want, by Elizabeth Crary • Young children share certain behaviors that are calculated to drive parents crazy. Here are hundreds of practical (and sometimes zany) ideas to help parents cope.
104 pages, ISBN 0-943990-79-3 paperback, 0-943990-80-7 library

Peekaboo and Other Games to Play with Your Baby, by Shari Steelsmith • Babies love games and this book is full of games they enjoy at different stages of development. All games help develop skills, are fun, and strengthen the bond between baby and parent.
96 pages, ISBN 0-943990-81-5 paperback, 0-943990-99-8 library

More books and ordering information on next page

Order these books for quick ideas

More books on preceding page. **Paperback, $9.95 each; library binding $18.95 each**

Joyful Play with Toddlers: Recipes for Fun with Odds and Ends, by Sandi Dexter • Toddlers at play are full of curiosity and daring. They need creative and safe ways to express themselves. Parents need lots of ideas for no-cost or low-cost toys, games, and activities.
128 pages, ISBN 1-884734-00-6 paperback, 1-884734-01-4 library

Taking Care of Me (So I Can Take Care of Others), by Barbara Carlson, Margaret Healy, Glo Wellman • By taking care of themselves, parents can take care of their children (and others) better. Learn how temperament, childhood experiences, basic needs, and goals affect parenting style.
128 pages, ISBN 1-884734-02-2 paperback, 1-884734-03-0 library

Ask for these books at your favorite bookstore, or call toll free 1-800-992-6657. VISA and MasterCard accepted with phone orders. Complete book catalog available on request.

Parenting Press, Inc., Dept. 404, P.O. Box 75267, Seattle, WA 98125
In Canada, call **Raincoast Books Distribution Co.,** 1-800-663-5714.
Prices subject to change without notice.